I love reading

Amazing Dinosaur Facts

by Leonie Bennett

Consultant: Dougal Dixon

Copyright © **ticktock Entertainment Ltd 2007**
First published in Great Britain in 2007 by **ticktock Media Ltd.,**
Unit 2, Orchard Business Centre, North Farm Road, Tunbridge Wells, Kent TN2 3XF

We would like to thank: Shirley Bickler and Suzanne Baker

ISBN 978 1 84696 609 5 pbk
Printed in China

Picture credits
t=top, b=bottom, c=centre, l-left, r=right, OFC= outside front cover
Lisa Alderson: 2, 9tl, 14bl, 15, 22b; John Alston: 14bc; Brian Edwards: 9bl, 10l, 10r,
23b; Natural History Museum: 5t, 7, 8; Luis Rey: 16-17, 20-21, 23t, 23c;
Shutterstock: 4l, 4r, 5b, 6l, 6r, 9tr, 9br, 10 background; Chris Tomlin: 1, 12-13, 18-19,
22t.

CONTENTS

The biggest dinosaur

Look at Supersaurus. It was probably the biggest dinosaur ever.

It was as heavy as 50 elephants.

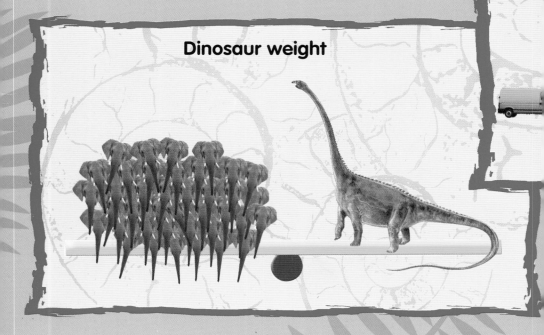

Dinosaur weight

It grew to 40 metres long. That's longer than eight vans.

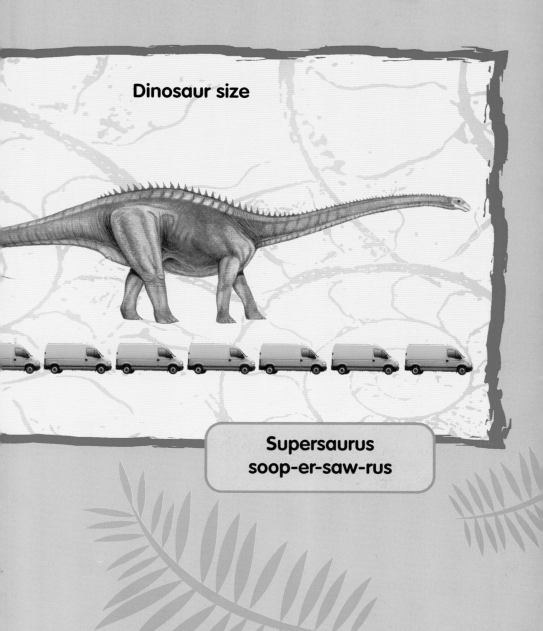

Dinosaur size

Supersaurus
soop-er-saw-rus

The smallest dinosaur

Look at Microraptor.

It was probably the smallest dinosaur.

Dinosaur size

It was as small as a chicken.

It had feathers on its arms, legs and tail.

It had long claws. It used its claws to hold on to trees.

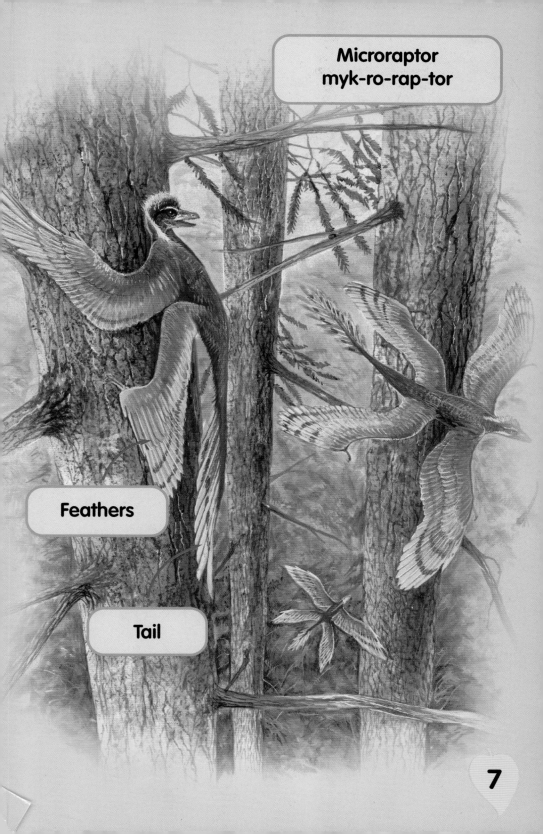

Microraptor
myk-ro-rap-tor

Feathers

Tail

Big head

This was probably the biggest meat-eating dinosaur.

Giganotosaurus
jie-gan-ot-o-sor-us

It was bigger than T. rex.

This dinosaur's head was as big
as a leopard.

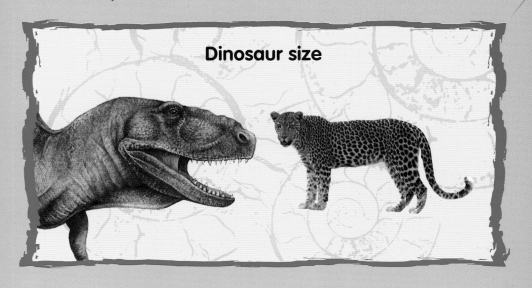

Dinosaur size

Some of its teeth were 15 centimetres long.

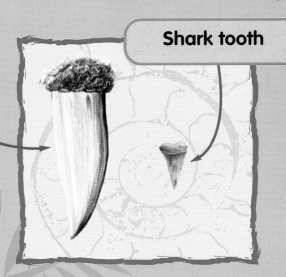

Shark tooth

**Giganotosaurus
tooth**

Big brain

Troodon was a small dinosaur but it had a big brain. It was probably the smartest dinosaur.

It had big eyes. It hunted for its food at night.

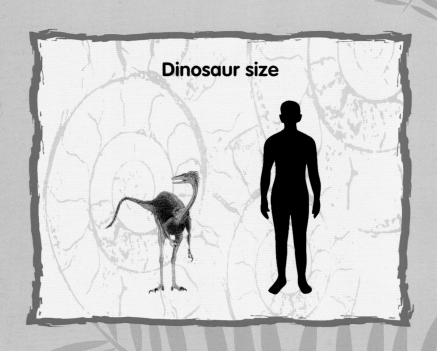

Dinosaur size

Troodon
troo-o-don

Eye

Keeping warm

Arizonasaurus was a kind of crocodile.

It lived at the same time as the dinosaurs.

The sail on its back helped to keep it warm.

It would turn around so the Sun was always shining on its sail.

Sun

Arizonasaurus
a-riz-o-na-sor-us

Sail

Little meat-eater

Eoraptor was one of the first meat-eating dinosaurs.

Meat-eating dinosaurs that lived after Eoraptor had the same body shape, but they were much bigger.

T. rex lived many years after Eoraptor. It looked like Eoraptor, but was much bigger!

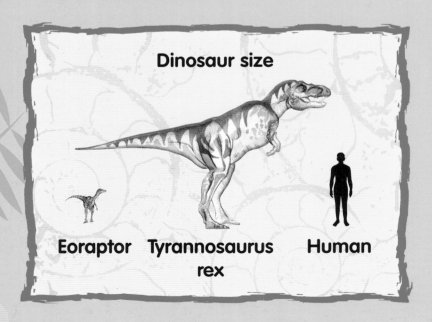

Dinosaur size

Eoraptor   Tyrannosaurus   Human
rex

Eoraptor was only one metre
tall.

Eoraptor
ee-o-rap-tor

Unusual head

This dinosaur had a crest on top of its head.

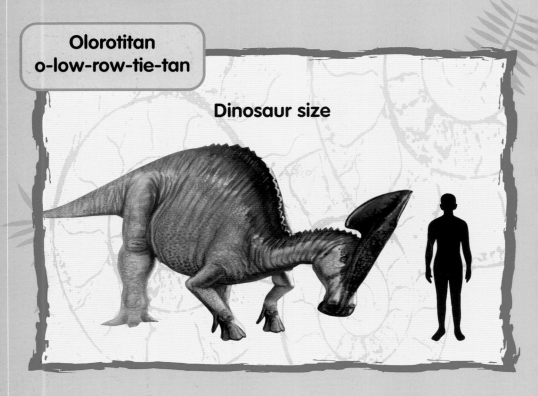

Olorotitan
o-low-row-tie-tan

Dinosaur size

It might have used the crest to make a loud sound.

The crest was shaped like a fan.

Olorotitan was about nine metres long.

Crest

The pterosaurs

Pterosaurs lived at the same time as dinosaurs.

They did not have feathers but some were covered with hair.

Pterosaurs' wings were made of skin and muscle.

Tail

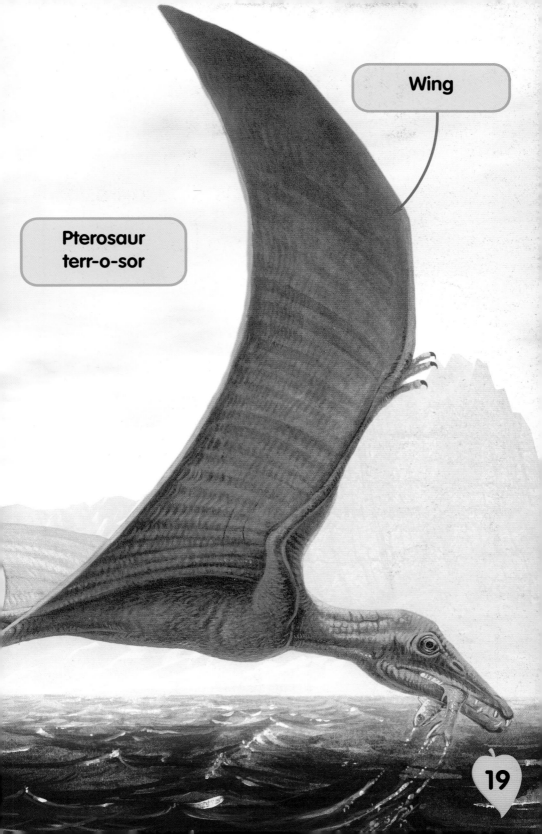

Wing

Pterosaur
terr-o-sor

19

Dinosaur in space

Coelophysis was a fast runner.

It ate small animals like lizards.

Coelophysis
see-lo-fie-sis

Astronauts took some Coelophysis bones on a space shuttle.

They thought it would be fun to take a dinosaur into space!

Thinking and talking about dinosaurs

Which dinosaur had a
sail on its back?

What did the sail
help it to do?

Was Giganotosaurus bigger or
smaller than T. rex?

Which dinosaur
had feathers?

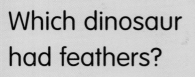

Which dinosaur
went to space?

Which dinosaur
looked like this
Eoraptor?

Activities

What did you think of this book?

 Brilliant **Good**  **OK**

Which page did you like best? Why?

• • • • • • • • • • • • • •

Make a sentence with these words:

eyes. • had • dinosaur • This • big

• • • • • • • • • • • • • •

Which dinosaur would you like to meet?
Why?

• • • • • • • • • • • • • •

Who is the author of this book?
Have you read *Hunting for Dinosaurs*
by the same author?